1

Natural Hair and the Law

Tracy Sanders, Esq.

P.O. Box 360764

Los Angeles, CA 90036

info@naturalhairandthelaw.com

Dedication

I dedicate this book to my darling family and friends.

I dedicate this book to all women of the African Diaspora.

Acknowledgments:

To Michelle Breyer, Naturally Curly, thanks for being an inspiration to the natural, curly, and textured hair community.

To Clarissa Davis-Ragland, Estrella Mountain Community College, thanks for providing a forum for me to present the Natural Hair and the Law Workshop during Black History Month.

To Ms. Waajid, Taliah Waajid Brand, thanks for providing a forum for me to present the Natural Hair and the Law Workshop at the World Natural Hair & Healthy Lifestyle Event.

Chapter 1

An Attorney's Life: Brown Girl, Nappy Hair, Kinky Hair

In this book, you will learn more about your rights, as an employee, to natural hair in the workplace. You will learn how employment discrimination law distinguishes natural hair such as an afro from natural hairstyles including braids, cornrows, twists, dreadlocks, and sisterlocks. The rights associated with natural hair may be protected by federal and state laws. An employer may, however, restrict natural hairstyles such as braids, cornrows, or dreadlocks through dress and grooming codes. These fine points will be explained including the various natural hair textures: straight, curly, or kinky. With respect to federal and state laws, rules may be applied differently due to factual circumstances.

The distinction between natural hair and natural hairstyles should demonstrate that legal issues related to natural hair in workplace are not always black and white. There are shades of gray. This means that your rights to natural hair in the workplace are not absolute.

Similarly, an employer does not have carte blanche authority to dictate your appearance, including natural hair. In the workplace, dress and grooming codes must be enforced in a race neutral manner to avoid lawsuits based on discrimination.

If you are an employee, I would like to commend you for taking an important step in protecting your rights to natural hair in the workplace. As an employer, it is beneficial to examine natural hair in the workplace to possibly avoid negative publicity and civil liability. Labor and management have a vested interested in knowing the law regarding natural hair in the workplace. While this conversation may be sensitive, knowledge about privileges and obligations may prevent workplace conflict.

First, knowledge of the law is empowering because it clears up ambiguity. Second, employers may discover that natural hair provides a sense of pride and cultural identity rather than a symbol of scorn or rebellion. Third, case studies will be examined, which should serve as a useful resource to avoid pitfalls. Finally, five tips will be provided to help you navigate natural hair in the workplace.

Why do I care deeply about natural hair and law? I am an African American woman who understands the struggle. The dichotomy of life as an American national of African descent has many layers: race, class, and natural hair, among others. These factors are quite interrelated. Like many African Americans, my ancestors arrived in the United States and endured forced immigration in the South. My ancestors landed in South Carolina and joined the enslaved population that contributed to the wealth of our nation. Yet, because of African roots, my ancestors did not legally share in the American pie. As a rule, they were considered African even if born on American soil. From a Eurocentric perspective, African heritage was inferior. An inferiority complex may linger in the psyche of some African Americans, which can be linked to slavery.

For me, the monologue begins with: "I am educated but my family is working class. I have traveled around the world and have great work experience. However, I am not really connected to wealthy influencers. Kudos, I am an attorney, but I wear a wig to conceal my difference – nappy hair, kinky hair!"

My life has been a continuous battle. I have fought to overcome an inferiority complex related to a working-class background, low self-esteem, and kinky hair. In my opinion, these three factors are correlated to success--or the lack of it--in the United States.

But nothing is set in stone. There are wealthy, universally beautiful people who have ruined their lives through poor choices. And there are those who started from humble beginnings, who were not perceived as overly attractive, who worked their way up to the C-Suite level. To assert, however, that appearance does not matter would be naïve.

For example, in the African American community, natural hair may be perceived as an indicator of social class. This is not a broad statement, but upper middle class and wealthy African Americans typically exude confidence and ease. The upper middle class and wealthy African Americans may be described as clean, modest, and light skinned with "good hair."

Some women in the African American community might have "good hair" as a result of genetics or higher income. Higher income provides the means to purchase top quality hair products, regular dermatologist appointments, and weekly salon visits. These are vital steps necessary to grow and maintain long, healthy hair. This statement is not to diminish anyone but merely to discuss how "good hair" may be connected to socio-economic status in the African American community.

Some scholars have linked social patterns in the African American community and the term "good hair" to slavery. During slavery, there were house slaves and field slaves. The house slaves were light skinned, had soft hair, and were better educated. After slavery ended, house slaves had more access to capital and opportunities. The family values may have been preserved through the years because of emphasis on legacy building through churches, higher education institutions, and marriage.

The field slaves closely resembled our African ancestors and were dark skinned, had hard hair, and were less educated. After slavery ended, field slaves had less access to capital and opportunities. The family values may have been devastated, resulting in broken families. Thus, class distinction in the African American community may have originated during slavery. Unfortunately, remnants of these social patterns are present today.

The observation of class distinction in the African American community with "good hair" as a correlating factor is not superficial or frivolous. It is a reality, particularly for those who have a link that closely resembles our African ancestry. The kinky hair that is growing out of our scalp serves as a constant reminder of a connection to Africa rather than to mainstream United States. African Americans without this noticeable link may assimilate easier into society, including the workplace.

While the African American community is not monolithic, I do believe that we are interconnected. We share a common history in the United States and must unify to promote social justice for all. It should be noted that attributes other than race, class, or physical characteristics contribute to achievement in our nation. Character, diligence, and integrity are noteworthy factors.

As for me, I have been able to overcome socio-economic barriers related to growing up as a brown-skinned girl with kinky hair in South Carolina. But feelings of inadequacy followed me to the Northeast. When I moved to New York, my life changed drastically, including the term for my natural hair texture. New York has a variety of African-descent communities–African, African American, Latin American, and Caribbean. There is a wide range of cultural differences and perspectives. In New York, I had been described as brown-skinned, dark skinned, and kinky haired. The labels that were assigned to me in the South–nappy haired, red-skinned, brown-skinned, or pecan tan were recycled in the Northeast--brown-skinned, dark-skinned, and kinky haired.

Even though I moved to New York from South Carolina, the migration felt like immigration. In some instances, I stood out as an African American with a subtle Southern accent. While it was difficult making the adjustment to New York, I had delightful friends who made the transition easier. They admired my courage to leave home in pursuit of a better life. Our friendships were rooted in humanity and an international sense of community. Through those relationships, I learned to accept myself and embrace Southern culture.

Regarding natural hairstyles in the workplace, I will begin with my life as a law student. During law school externships, the goals were to gain practical work experience and earn wages. I did not have any negative incidents as a result of natural hairstyles such as braids or twists. The employers may have been content with my appearance because it was seasonal employment.

I enjoyed wearing natural hairstyles during freezing, cold winters in Syracuse. I would endure the five-hour trip to New York City for hair salon visits. Now I realize that my legal career began on the first day of law school. Perhaps wearing natural hairstyles was not the best presentation at law school or in the workplace, based on normative grooming standards.

However, I had a wonderful learning experience during law school. I went to law school and achieved the long-term goals of graduating and passing the bar exam. I think that the innermost concerns about my appearance lingered even though I did it—made it in law school! I have finally overcome insecurity through a keen interest in personal development, professional development, and daily affirmations. Consequently, I have attracted aspirational friends, beloved supporters, and amazing career opportunities!

After law school, I did not wear natural hairstyles as a new attorney. To fit in, I wore weaves and wigs to conceal my natural hair. This grooming strategy may flourish or flounder, depending on the employer. In academia or a public interest legal environment, natural hair and natural hairstyles may be acceptable. In a corporate environment, however, dress and grooming codes are more restrictive. Natural hair and natural hairstyles are often deemed unprofessional. Corporate employers are cognizant of business image. There could be concerns about client interaction and potential loss of profit due to perceptions about employees.

For example, in some upper class or wealthy environments regardless of race, "black hair" – natural hair and natural hairstyles -- may be perceived as poor, dirty, or unprofessional. What can I say? There are unspoken rules in society and if you do not fit in with the establishment, your employment situation may be difficult. If you are going to "rock" natural hair and natural hairstyles, especially in a corporate work environment, you must have confidence.

Most employers seek the best candidates and want a happy, productive work environment. Generally, performance, emotional intelligence, and business relationships are keys to success in the workplace. But could natural hair and natural hairstyles determine whether you will receive a yes or no from a potential employer? Yes. Promotion? Yes.

With all qualifications being equal, appearance may be a crucial factor, particularly for women in the United States. For women, appearance may be viewed as a source of feminine power. Some men are instantly mesmerized by women with long, flowing tresses in the workplace. Women may often esteem other women colleagues with naturally beautiful hair. Does this equate to a competitive advantage? Probably. Is this fair? No. Should you allow appearance to determine your worth? No.

I refuse to accept that anyone is superior because of genetic variances such as natural hair, skin, or any other immutable characteristic. All women hurt, laugh, cry, eat, sleep, and love regardless of appearance. Accordingly, women should encourage each other and collaborate to achieve common goals.

Through the years, I have learned to accept mistakes from the past, love myself in the present, and hope for the best in the future. Every challenge that we face provides an opportunity to help someone else. Perchance the insecurity about my natural hair caused me to become passionate about legal issues related to natural hair in the workplace. Since I am dedicated to the topic, I am excited about sharing my natural hair journey and legal background with you.

Chapter 2

What is Employment Discrimination Law?

Employment discrimination law protects against disparate treatment due to natural hair, which may occur in the workplace or schools. This book will focus on natural hair in the workplace and your rights and obligations as an employee. You will learn more about federal and state employment discrimination laws. Before discussing employment discrimination laws in greater detail, it is important to explore the meaning of natural hair.

There are various types of hair textures: straight, curly, or kinky. Although there are variations, hair texture differentiates racial groups. For example, typically straight hair is linked to people of European or Asian descent, curly hair is linked to people of Latin American or Middle Eastern descent, and kinky hair is linked to people of African descent.

In the African, African American, Caribbean, and Latin American cultures, natural hair is the unaltered hair texture at birth. Natural hair may be styled as an afro, braids, cornrows, twists, sisterlocks, or dreadlocks.

In the United States, most people work to make a living and thrive. Earned income provides a means to cover household expenses, provide for our families, afford medical care, and save for retirement. Without earned income, it would be nearly impossible for most of us to meet our basic needs. Therefore, the ability to seek and maintain gainful employment is critical.

The hiring process usually involves an application, phone screening, and job interview. If you are preparing for a job interview, there might be apprehension that your afro, braids, cornrows, twists, sisterlocks, or dreadlocks may prevent you from getting the job. If you are already employed, it might take a while for you to transition into a natural hairstyle due to fear of retaliation. Justifiably so, since there have been cases where natural hairstyles have resulted in candidates not being hired or employees being fired. Recently, a federal court held that an employer may ban a natural hairstyle, dreadlocks, in the workplace.

Please review the hypotheticals below and write down your feelings about each scenario.

Hypothetical 1: News Reporter or Columnist?

Kristina Maverick earned a journalism degree in college. Ms. Maverick was a vegan, practiced yoga, and made a commitment to maintain her natural hair, an afro. Ms. Maverick straightened her afro with a flat iron for job interviews due to concerns about discrimination. After several job interviews, Ms. Maverick had two employment offers. Ms. Maverick considered employment as a news reporter at a TV station or columnist at a Black owned newspaper. She researched both employers carefully before making a final decision. After seeing photos online of current employees at the TV station, Ms. Maverick concluded that her afro might be problematic as a news reporter. Therefore, she began her journalism career as a columnist at a Black owned newspaper. She proudly wears her afro to work and speaks out about self-care.

Explanation

Possibly you are from a different culture and do not have to think about your natural hair before going on a job interview. Or you may think that focusing on natural hair in the workplace is irrelevant. In fact, some African descent people are born with straight hair and might have the same perspective. But for naturalistas who must make a choice about natural hair, natural hairstyles, or gainful employment, it is truly a dilemma.

The decision about whether to wear natural hair or a natural hairstyle in certain workspaces requires serious deliberation. You may have to balance freedom of expression, cultural identity, and gainful employment. The stakes are high as appearance in the workplace may be a factor in hiring, firing, promotion, harassment, training, wages, or benefits.

Hypothetical 2: Executive Assistant, Job Applicant #86914

Jan Newberry, an African American female, had been conducting a job search for three months. She applied for an executive-assistant position at an accounting firm. After a telephone screening, she was invited to a job interview at the accounting firm. Ms. Newberry usually wears a natural hairstyle, cornrows, but chose a wig for the job interview.

Explanation

The intersection of natural hair in the workplace presents several legal issues for employees and employers. Let's discuss the legal issues, examine federal and state laws, apply this knowledge to case studies, and conclude with five tips to help you navigate natural hair in the workplace.

Chapter 3

Federal Law-Title VII of the Civil Rights Act of 1964

Title VII of the Civil Rights Act of 1964 (Title VII) prohibits discrimination in the workplace when two requirements are satisfied. First, the employee must belong to a protected class as listed below. Second, the federal statute covers employers including business organizations with 15 or more employees, government organizations, labor unions, and employment agencies. Under these circumstances, the U.S. Equal Employment Opportunity Community ("EEOC"), a federal agency, has the authority to enforce Title VII and investigate employment discrimination claims.

According to the EEOC, Title VII prohibits employment discrimination based on the following factors:

- Race (including physical characteristics such as hair or facial features)

- Color (pigmentation, complexion, or skin shade)

- Religion (religious, ethical, or moral beliefs)

- Sex (including pregnancy, and in limited cases gender identity and sexual orientation)

- National Origin (place of origin or ancestry)

- Age (40 or older)

- Disability (history of disability, physical impairment, or mental impairment)

- Genetic Information (individual or family members genetic test results).

Title VII prohibits discrimination in the workplace based on race, which is tied to physical characteristics such as hair or facial features. Title VII does, however, allow employers to establish dress and grooming codes. The dress and grooming codes must be neutral, adopted without discriminatory intent, and applied consistently to all racial and ethnic groups. When dress and grooming codes are adopted without discriminatory intent but have a disparate impact, they may be enforced, but only if necessary for legitimate business purposes.

Sample Grooming Policy – Not in Violation of Title VII

Hair must be clean, neat, and a conservative color so that it will not hinder vision or performance. Long hair must be pulled back and not cause a safety hazard. Contact of hair with hands if working in food service must be prevented. To avoid contact with food, hair must be restrained by a hair net.

Chapter 4

Title VII and African American Hair/Black Hair/Kinky Hair

A significant proportion of the language in the EEOC Compliance Manual Section 15, Race & Color Discrimination, specifically cites to discrimination against African Americans. This may be due, in part, because (1) Title VII originated as a result of the Civil Rights Movement of the 1950s and 1960s and (2) African American hair, Black hair, or kinky hair texture is disproportionately affected by adverse employment action in the workplace. In Chapter 6, we will review actual natural hair and natural hairstyle discrimination cases.

The catalyst for Title VII and the EEOC derived from the Civil Rights Movement, primarily in Southern states. African Americans and civil rights activists across the nation challenged oppression, disenfranchisement, discrimination, and segregation in the United States. Civil rights activists urged the United States government to enact legislation such as Title VII, the Voting Rights Act of 1965, and the Civil Rights Act of 1968. Title VII had been enacted to end discriminatory practices against African Americans. Congress widened the protection to any person, regardless of race or color.

Pursuant to the EEOC Compliance Manual ("Manual"), Section 15 VII-B5 Appearance and Grooming Standards, employers may establish hairstyle rules in the workplace. The Manual requires the following conditions when establishing hairstyle rules to prevent discrimination in the workplace:

- ❖ Reasonable expectation that hair should be neat, clean, and groomed

- ❖ Respect for racial differences in hair textures (straight/curly/kinky)

- ❖ Consistent application to all racial and ethnic groups

- ❖ Not unduly deterrent to African American/Black hair/kinky hair

Title VII prohibits discrimination based on African American/Black hair/kinky hair or natural hair that complies with the Manual. Title VII does not forbid employers from banning natural hairstyles. The legal reasoning to exclude natural hairstyles from protection is the distinction between immutable and mutable physical characteristics. An immutable physical characteristic, such as an afro growing out of your scalp, cannot be changed. A mutable physical characteristic, such as natural hairstyles like braids, cornrows, twists, sisterlocks, or dreadlocks can be changed.

Natural hair, an afro, has been tied to race by the courts because it is a product of natural growth from the human body. The judiciary has the authority to determine the scope of race pursuant to Title VII. According to the judiciary, Title VII does not define race, but there has been interpretation by case law. Race has been construed through case law as an immutable physical characteristic. An immutable physical characteristic is one that is unchangeable and evident, like skin color or natural hair. Thus, race is a protected category.

The federal courts have determined that unlike natural hair, natural hairstyles are mutable characteristics that can be changed and worn by anyone regardless of genetics. Since natural hairstyles are considered cultural connections not tied to race, there is no protection from employment discrimination through Title VII. Therefore, employers may ban natural hairstyles and not be subjected to civil liability imposed by Title VII.

Chapter 5

The CROWN ACT: State Laws

The public broadcast of a white police officer kneeling on the neck of a Black man, George Floyd, until he died, along with several other incendiary and unjustified killings of Black Americans by police, opened the eyes of many people to the discrimination faced daily by Blacks in America. Even though civil rights laws have existed since 1964, African Americans who were fired from jobs or expelled from school programs because of their natural hair and natural hairstyles have lost discrimination lawsuits because existing laws did not specifically cover natural hairstyles such as braids, locs, twists, and bantu knots. The current civil rights laws only cover natural hair but not natural hairstyles. These natural hairstyles were often labeled "unprofessional" by employers. And since courts ruled that natural hairstyle are not tied to race, courts found no discrimination on the part of the employers.

In reaction to this unfair treatment and recognizing that Congress failed to enact protection against discrimination based on natural hair or natural hairstyles, many state legislators and city council members introduced The CROWN Act in their jurisdictions. The CROWN ACT means Create a Respectful and Open World for Natural Hair prohibits discrimination based on natural hair and natural hairstyles. As of March 2021, eight states and several cities or counties have enacted various versions of The CROWN Act.

This chapter introduces readers to jurisdictions where The CROWN Act has become law in the United States. The CROWN Act has created a vision of hope that has led to legislation, which provides a path to freedom from natural hair discrimination. This vision is taking hold slowly but surely across the nation. This chapter lists states, cities, and counties where The CROWN Act has passed, where it is being considered, and where it has been proposed but rejected.

States Where The CROWN Act Has Become Law

California

The first CROWN Act was enacted in 2019 in California. State Senator Holly Mitchell, a Democrat and member of the California Black Legislative Caucus, introduced the bill, and Governor Gavin Newsome signed it into law on July 3, 2019. Sen. Mitchell had served in the California State Assembly before being elected to the California Senate. She has since become a member of the Los Angeles County Board of Supervisors.

Senator Mitchell's 2019 bill, S.B. 188, titled "Discrimination: Hairstyles," was informally known as the "Creating a Respectful and Open Workplace for Natural Hair Act," or by the acronym "The CROWN Act." It amended sections of the California Education code and the Fair Employment and Housing Act on discrimination. The California Legislative Counsel's Digest explained that the bill would expand the definition of race for purposes of discrimination to include "traits historically associated with race, including, but not limited to, hair texture and protective hairstyles, and would define protective hairstyles for purposes of these provisions." Section 1 of the bill sets forth seven declarations, among them, these three:

"(e) Federal courts accept that Title VII of the Civil Rights Act of 1964 prohibits discrimination based on race, and therefore protects against discrimination against afros. However, the courts do not understand that afros are not the only natural presentation of Black hair. Black hair can also be naturally presented in braids, twists, and locks.

(f) In a society in which hair has historically been one of many determining factors of a person's race, and whether they were a second-class citizen, hair today remains a proxy for race. Therefore, hair discrimination targeting hairstyles associated with race is racial discrimination.

(g) Acting in accordance with the constitutional values of fairness, equity, and opportunity for all, the Legislature recognizes that continuing to enforce a Eurocentric image of professionalism through purportedly race-neutral grooming policies that disparately impact Black individuals and exclude them from some workplaces is in direct opposition to equity and opportunity for all."

In other words, no longer can a person lawfully be discriminated against in California for wearing a natural hairstyle.

The reasoning in the California Legislative Counsel's Digest justified amending two sections of California law to give students, employees, and people seeking housing a path forward in the face of perceived discrimination based on how they choose to wear their hair. Section 2 of the California Senate bill amended the existing Education code so that the definition of "race" now includes "protective hairstyles" such as "braids, locks, and twists" as "traits historically associated with race" that warrant protection from discrimination. See California Education Code § 212.1. Section 3 of the bill amended the Government Code, section 12926, which covers employment and housing. It now includes a reference to hair in the definition of race:

"(w) 'Race' is inclusive of traits historically associated with race, including, but not limited to, hair texture and protective hairstyles.

(x) 'Protective hairstyles' includes, but is not limited to, such hairstyles as braids, locks, and twists." See California Government Code § 12926.

Under the California CROWN Act, employers can still make and enforce certain policies, but only if they affect all employees or housing applicants the same as those with natural hairstyles. Employers can still require workers to secure their hair for hygiene or safety reasons--in the food service or construction industries, for example. These "bona fide occupational qualifications" must make sense in the workplace and should not be arbitrary requirements.

New York

New York State also added The CROWN Act protections to its Education code and Human Rights Law in 2019. New York had enacted The Dignity for All Students Act ("Dignity Act") in 2010 to prevent bullying and discrimination and provide a safe and supportive environment "free from discrimination, intimidation, taunting, harassment, and bullying on school property, a school bus, and/or at a school function." In short, the goal of the Dignity Act was to encourage dignity and respect for all.

Building on the Dignity Act's foundation, in 2019 Democratic State Senator Jamaal T. Bailey and Assembly member Tremaine S. Wright co-sponsored legislation, Senate Bill 6209A and Assembly Bill 7797A, to update the Dignity Act to include in the definition of race "traits historically associated with race, including but not limited to, hair texture and protective hairstyles," such as "braids, locks, and twists." The legislation also amended the New York Human Rights Act, which provides protection from discrimination in the workplace.

Governor Andrew Cuomo signed the Assembly bill into law on July 12, 2019, as Chapter 95. In a statement issued that day, Gov. Cuomo wrote: "For much of our nation's history, people of color - particularly women - have been marginalized and discriminated against simply because of their hair style or texture. By signing this bill into law, we are taking an important step toward correcting that history and ensuring people of color are protected from all forms of discrimination."

Like the California CROWN Act, the New York legislation amended existing anti-discrimination laws to include references to some protective hairstyles, including "braids, locks, and twists" and other natural hairstyles. These updated definitions were added to section 292 of the New York Human Rights Law and section 11 of the state's Dignity for All Students Act. As in California, no judicial opinions have yet been published involving the natural hair updates to these New York State laws.

New Jersey

New Jersey gained negative notoriety in 2018 when a white referee for a high school wrestling match gave a young mixed-race athlete ninety seconds to make a choice: either cut his locs or forfeit the match. The young man reluctantly allowed a coach to cut his locs, in front of the audience assembled in the gym. One year later, on December 19, 2019, in response to this humiliating discriminatory display, the New Jersey legislature passed The CROWN Act.

New Jersey's CROWN Act amends the New Jersey Law Against Discrimination so that the term "race" includes "traits historically associated with race, including hair texture, hair type and protective hairstyles." See 11 N.J. Statute § 10:5-5; *see also* McKnight, Reynolds-Jackson, Speight & Timberlake Bill to Prohibit Hair Discrimination Advances in Assembly. In signing Assembly Bill A-5564 into law, Governor Phil Murphy stated that "no one should be made to feel uncomfortable or be discriminated against because of their natural hair." The law applies to the workplace as well as to schools and public accommodations.

Colorado

In early March 2020, Colorado enacted its own CROWN Act, House Bill 1048. The bill summary explains, "The act enacts the 'Creating a Respectful and Open World for Natural Hair Act of 2020,' also known as the 'CROWN Act of 2020,' which specifies that, for purposes of anti-discrimination laws in the context of public education, employment practices, housing, public accommodations, and advertising, protections against discrimination on the basis of one's race include hair texture, hair type, or a protective hairstyle commonly or historically associated with race, such as braids, locs, twists, tight coils or curls, cornrows, Bantu knots, Afros, and headwraps." Colorado's law refers in detail to more natural hairstyles than other state laws, and it applies to advertising as well as schools, workplaces, and public accommodations.

"When someone chooses to celebrate their natural hair, we should join them in that celebration and not discriminate against them," Representative Leslie Herod, a sponsor of the bill, told the Denver Post when the Colorado CROWN Act was passed.

Washington

Additionally, in 2020, Washington State passed House Bill 2602 banning hair discrimination. Representative Melanie Morgan sponsored the bill and, in a statement on the House Democrats' page noted its positive message, especially for children with natural hair: "The way we choose to style our hair is culturally meaningful, and it has no impact on our abilities to show up professionally, hygienically, and naturally at work and school. We are sending a message to our children, 'You are beautiful just the way you are.'"

The Washington state law adds legal protection for "locks, braids, afros, twists, and protective hair coverings" under Washington's existing racial discrimination laws.

Virginia

In April 2020, Virginia became the first southern state to enact a version of The CROWN Act that allows a school board to include "a dress or grooming code" in its code of conduct. The law, House Bill No. 837 (Chapter 0678), took effect on July 1, 2020, and provided guidelines for student dress or grooming codes: "Any dress or grooming code included in a school board's code of student conduct or otherwise adopted by a school board shall (i) permit any student to wear any religiously, ethnically, or culturally specific or significant head covering or hairstyle, including hijabs, yarmulkes, headwraps, braids, locs, and cornrows...."

Although the Virginia CROWN Act applies only in educational settings, not in the workplace or public accommodations, it aims to prevent discrimination in schools based on, among other things, natural hairstyles, including braids, locs, and cornrows. In an interview with CNN, Governor Ralph Northam stated that sending children home from school "because their hair looks a certain way," constitutes discrimination. "This is not only unacceptable and wrong; it is not what we stand for in Virginia." Although narrow in its protections, Virginia's CROWN Act protection for school children and teens is a good start for a state with a long history of racial discrimination. However, the law is not mandatory— a school board may choose not to have any grooming policy in its code of conduct, and in that case, there would be no legal protection in place for natural hairstyles.

Maryland

The CROWN Act became law in Maryland in May 2020, without the Governor's signature. It had been the law in Montgomery County, Maryland, before the legislature adopted it statewide. House Bill 1444 (Chapter 473) added definitions of "protective hairstyle" --to include "braids, twists, and locks"--to eleven titles including housing, employment, and public accommodations. The definition of "race" now includes "traits associated with race, including hair texture, afro hairstyles, and protective hairstyles."

Connecticut

In early March 2021, Connecticut's state legislators passed The CROWN Act by a unanimous vote. Governor Ned Lamont then made the state the eighth in the country to prohibit natural hair discrimination. He signed into law House Bill No. 6515, The CROWN Act, which amends Connecticut's anti-discrimination laws to define race as "inclusive of ethnic traits historically associated with race, including, but not limited to, hair texture and protective hairstyles." Connecticut's CROWN Act defines protective hairstyles as including but not limited to "wigs, headwraps, and hairstyles such as individual braids, cornrows, locs, twists, Bantu knots, afros, and afro puffs." Connecticut's CROWN Act applies to all anti-discrimination laws in the state.

Some States That Are Considering The CROWN Act

Several states have considered various versions of The CROWN Act in 2020 and 2021 but have not yet enacted the law. These states include Mississippi, which would have added protective hairstyles to anti-discrimination laws in the workplace, schools, and school districts; Oklahoma, which would have protected employees at work; Georgia, whose two bills would offer natural hair protection in schools and workplaces and, in the second bill, in housing and public accommodations; Florida, which would offer protection from housing discrimination; Louisiana, which would prevent discrimination in the workplace but not in schools; Missouri and Alabama, whose bills would have afforded protection only in schools; Ohio, which would have covered private as well as public schools; West Virginia; Illinois; Massachusetts; and others.

In August of 2020, Nebraska's Governor Pete Rickets vetoed CROWN Act legislation introduced by State Senator Machaela Cavanaugh, LB 1060. Her bill would have amended Nebraska's Fair Employment Practice Act. Ricketts stated in his veto letter that the bill needed "to add protections for employees based upon their immutable hair texture and to also add protections for employers centered on health and safety standards." Senator Terrell McKinney introduced a newer version in January 2021; as of March, the bill has not yet passed in Nebraska. The bill was amended to address Governor Ricketts' concerns, however, so if it does make it through the legislative process, he should have no reason to veto it.

West Virginia came very close to enacting The CROWN Act in 2020 after the story of a young wrestler who was forced to cut his locs to participate in a wrestling match went viral. However, a legislative committee voted to discharge the bill, SB 850, meaning that they refused to vote on it, and it died. In March 2021, the city council in Charleston, West Virginia, passed a resolution supporting The CROWN Act and urging the state legislature to end natural hair discrimination. However, the legislature has not made enactment a priority.

Cities and Counties That Have Enacted The CROWN Act

Even though The CROWN Act has stalled in many State legislatures, some city councils and county boards have voted to adopt versions of it. As of March 2021, these cities and counties include the following:

- Albuquerque, NM

- Tucson, AZ

- Kansas City, MO

- Clayton County and Stockbridge, GA

- Broward County, FL

- Cincinnati, OH

- Covington, KE

- Morgantown, WV

Summary

The CROWN Act is necessary supplement to the Civil Rights Act of 1964, but it is the law in only eight states. It is hard to believe that in the third decade of the twenty-first century, employers, school administrators, coaches, landlords, and others in forty-two states may still discriminate based on a hairstyle associated with a particular race.

Ideally, the United States Congress will enact a CROWN Act that will apply across the country. But until that happens, contacting your state legislators and urging them to support The CROWN Act is the best step to take.

Chapter 6

Now it is your turn! Since you have learned more about federal, state, and local employment discrimination laws, apply your knowledge. Here are case studies related to natural hair and natural hairstyles in the workplace.

Employment Discrimination Case Studies

Case Study 1 – Finger Waves and Ponytail

Kandy Furman is a machine operator at Glas9 with an excellent employment record. She reports to work on time, gets along well with others, and completes duties as instructed by the company's guidelines. Ms. Furman likes to wear her hair in natural hairstyles. She does not have a relaxer, which is a chemical to straighten curly or kinky hair. One week, Ms. Furman came to work with finger waves. Glas9's dress and grooming codes require employees to have neat and well-groomed hairstyles that do not cause a safety hazard. During a break, Ms. Furman's supervisor, Jake Brunson, informed her that the finger waves hairstyle was "unacceptable." He stated it was "different." Mr. Brunson admitted that the finger waves hairstyle was neat, well groomed, and did not present a safety hazard. However, he alleged that the finger waves hairstyle was too "eye catching" and "inappropriate." Ms. Furman had been warned that she should inform management before changing hairstyles. Ms. Furman had been required to bring a picture to work for approval in advance.

Two weeks later, Ms. Furman came to work with a ponytail. Mr. Brunson informed Ms. Furman that she had violated the agreement to get permission before changing hairstyles. Mr. Brunson stated the ponytail was "fancy" and "unacceptable" because it "called too much attention" to her in the workplace. Ms. Furman thereafter filed a complaint with the EEOC. Do you think that Ms. Furman has a valid employment discrimination claim?

Case Study 1 – Finger Waves and Ponytail

Explanation

Ms. Furman presented a disparate treatment claim and there is evidence of unlawful employment discrimination. Here, Mr. Brunson violated Title VII by preventing Ms. Furman from wearing finger waves, a ponytail, and other hairstyles that he perceived as "eye catching," "fancy," or "unacceptable." There is no indication that Ms. Furman violated Glas9's dress and grooming code. Ms. Furman was required to submit pictures of any hairstyle she wanted to wear and get approval from her manager, but no other employees were required to do this. Mr. Brunson restricted Ms. Furman's hairstyles while failing to subject other employees of different races to the same standard.

See *Hollins v. Atlantic Co.*, 188 F.3d 652 (6th Cir. 1999), and *Jenkins v. Blue Cross Mutual Hospital Insurance, Inc.*, 538 F.2d 164 (7th Cir. 1976).

Case Study 2 - Cornrows

LaReatha Clark has been employed by Starlight Airlines as an airport gate agent for ten years. Her duties include extensive customer contact such as greeting passengers, issuing tickets, issuing boarding passes, and checking luggage. As a result of Ms. Clark's position, she is prohibited from wearing natural hairstyles like braids or cornrows. Ms. Clark started attending natural hair meetups and decided she wanted to wear cornrows. Ms. Clark believes that she has a right to wear cornrows as a Black woman. She thinks that Starlight Airline's grooming policy discriminates against Black people pursuant to Title VII. Title VII prohibits workplace discrimination based on race. Ms. Clark thinks that banning cornrows violates Title VII because cornrow is a Black hairstyle. She feels that her natural hairstyle, cornrows, are connected to African American culture. Assuming the case proceeds to litigation, how would the court rule in this matter?

Case Study 2 - Cornrows

Explanation

Ms. Clark does not have a sustainable Title VII claim. The court would dismiss Ms. Clark's claim because the hairstyle regulation prohibiting all braiding hairstyles does not have an adverse effect on employment opportunity at the company--it does not regulate because of any immutable characteristic. An immutable characteristic is a physical trait that someone is born with or that cannot be altered. This means, for example, unaltered natural hair. The cornrows are an artificial hairstyle rather than natural hair. Ms. Clark could change the cornrows, as they are an artifice that does not grow out of her scalp. The hairstyle regulation is a ban on cornrows, a hairstyle, rather than on Ms. Clark's natural hair. Ms. Clark failed to comply with Starlight Airline's dress and grooming code.

Starlight Airline's dress and grooming code is not intended to discriminate against Black women. Even though the hairstyle regulation may have a disparate impact on Black women or men who desire to wear cornrows, the company may be concerned about business image and may therefore restrict natural hairstyles. In commenting on this topic, the EEOC explained that employers "can impose neutral hairstyle rules –

e.g., that hair be neat, clean, and well-groomed – as long as the rules

respect racial differences in hair textures and are applied evenhandedly."

EEOC Compliance Manual 15-VII (B)(5), Appearance and Grooming

Standards.

Ms. Clark's position as an airport gate agent involved extensive

customer contact. Furthermore, the hairstyle regulation applies equally

to all racial and ethnic groups. Therefore, the hairstyle regulation is not

discriminatory merely because most women who wear cornrows are

Black women.

See *Rogers v. American Airlines,* 527 F. Supp. 229 (S.D.N.Y. 1981).

Case Study – Dreadlocks

Tameka Wilson, an African American woman, completed an application and group interview for a customer service representative position at the Goodyear Insurance Company. Ms. Wilson took pride in keeping her blond dreadlocks neat and clean. Ms. Wilson was one of the candidates selected for employment after the group interview. Sharon Bailey, the human resources manager, congratulated Ms. Wilson and welcomed her to the company. Ms. Bailey informed Ms. Wilson that the company does not allow dreadlocks and she must cut them off before the first day of work. Ms. Wilson declined to cut her dreadlocks. Ms. Bailey rescinded the employment offer. Ms. Wilson filed a claim with the EEOC based on race discrimination due to her dreadlocks.

1. Can the EEOC file a lawsuit on Ms. Wilson's behalf in court?

2. Would the United States District Court for the Southern District of Alabama dismiss Ms. Wilson's race discrimination claim?

3. Would the United States Court of Appeals for the Eleventh Circuit dismiss Ms. Wilson's race discrimination claim?

4. Would the United States Supreme Court hear this case?

Case Study 3 – Dreadlocks
Explanation

1. Can the EEOC file a lawsuit on Ms. Wilson's behalf in court?

Yes, the EEOC can file a lawsuit on Ms. Wilson's behalf in court and argue that rescinding the employment offer constituted illegal discrimination in violation of Title VII. Ms. Wilson or any African American person should not suffer diminished employment opportunities due to a natural hairstyle specific to a racial or ethnic group.

See *EEOC v. Catastrophe Management Solutions*, 11 F. Supp. 3d 1139 (S.D. Ala. 2014), and the appellate ruling that affirmed it, No. 14-13482 (11th Cir. Sept. 15, 2016).

2. Would the United States District Court for the Southern District of Alabama dismiss Ms. Wilson's race discrimination claim?

The United States District Court for the Southern District of Alabama would rule against the EEOC and dismiss Ms. Wilson's race discrimination claim.

In a similar case, the Alabama District Court ruled that the employer's grooming policy restricting dreadlocks did not violate Title VII (42 U.S.C. § 2000e). The court reasoned that grooming codes that exclude natural hairstyles are not discriminatory if the hairstyle can be changed, like cornrows or dreadlocks. Even if a natural hairstyle is closely associated with a race or ethnicity, it is a mutable characteristic not protected by Title VII. Title VII protection based on race discrimination is limited to immutable characteristics, those that cannot be changed. The Alabama District Court refused to expand Title VII's scope of immutable characteristics to include socio-cultural racial significance such as natural hairstyles. Therefore, an employer could ban dreadlocks.

See *EEOC v. Catastrophe Management Solutions*, No. 13-00476-CB-M, 2014 WL 47758 (S.D. Ala. Mar. 27, 2014) and the appellate court ruling that affirmed it, No. 14-13482 (Sept. 15, 2016).

3. Would the United States Court of Appeals for the Eleventh Circuit dismiss Ms. Wilson's race discrimination claim?

The United States Court of Appeals for the Eleventh Circuit would rule in favor of Goodyear Insurance Company and uphold the Alabama District Court ruling that an employer can ban dreadlocks. In a similar case, the Eleventh Circuit rejected the EEOC's assertion that race is a social construct and should not be limited to immutable characteristics. Although Title VII does not define "race," jurisprudence has defined it as immutable characteristics existing through ancestry, descent, or heredity--in other words, a feature someone is born with. The Eleventh Circuit reasoned that race should be interpreted according to the current legal standard. Any change to the meaning of race pursuant to Title VII must be enacted by Congress, not changed by a court. (Title VII does not define the term "race.") Since dreadlocks are a natural hairstyle that can be altered rather than an immutable characteristic tied to race (for example, kinky hair), the Eleventh Circuit would dismiss Ms. Wilson's race discrimination claim.

See *EEOC v. Catastrophe Management Solutions*, No. 14-13482 (11th Cir. Sept. 15, 2016, denying rehearing en banc Dec. 5, 2017).

5. Will the United States Supreme Court hear this case?

No, the United States Supreme Court declined to hear a similar case about dreadlocks in the workplace.

(See the May 4, 2018 article at the NAACP's Legal Defense and Education Fund's site: https://www.naacpldf.org/press-release/u-s-supreme-court-declines-review-major-employment-discrimination-case-targeting-natural-black-hairstyles/).

Case Study 4 – Braids

Cara Greene is an attorney who recently returned to the job market after staying at home with her children for three years. She was hired by Legal Discovery, a temporary employment agency. Legal Discovery has a grooming policy that includes "no braided hairstyles." Ms. Greene wears a variety of braided hairstyles. After accepting a new contract with Legal Discovery, Ms. Greene complained to the human resources manager that the grooming policy is discriminatory. Ms. Greene alleged that it would screen out a disproportionate percentage of Black candidates. Shortly after complaining about the grooming policy, Legal Discovery fired Ms. Greene. Ms. Greene filed a complaint with the EEOC for retaliatory discharge. Assuming the case proceeds to litigation, how should the court rule in this matter?

Case Study 4 - Braids

Explanation

Legal Discovery would prevail against the retaliatory discharge claim because the "no braided hairstyles" restriction in the grooming policy is not prohibited under Title VII. Case law clearly states that natural hairstyles such as braids are voluntary aesthetic choices not protected by Title VII. The judiciary has defined race as a protected class under Title VII, which includes immutable physical characteristics. Immutable characteristics include hair growing out of your scalp, or unique facial features. Voluntary aesthetic choices are not a part of race as defined by Title VII. As such, Title VII does not forbid discrimination based on natural hairstyles. Therefore, Legal Discovery lawfully terminated Ms. Greene for challenging the grooming policy.

See *McBride v. Lawstaf, Inc.*, No. 1:96-CV-0196-CC, 1996 U.S. Dist. LEXIS 16190, 1996 WL 755779, 71 Fair Empl. Prac. Cas. (BNA) 1758 (N.D. Ga. 1996).

Chapter 7

Five Tips for Employees with Natural Hair, Natural Hairstyles, and Protective-Hairstyles in the Workplace

1. **<u>Follow Dress and Grooming Codes</u>:**

   Pay attention to your current or prospective employer's culture consisting of work environment, mission, values, expectations, and goals. Read and understand the current or prospective employer's dress and grooming codes. While dress and grooming codes should not violate state or federal laws, restrictions are allowed. An employer may require that hair must be neat, clean, and well groomed, and that it does not present a safety hazard. Remember the distinction between natural hair (immutable--cannot be altered and is possibly protected by Title VII) and natural hairstyles (mutable--may be altered and possibly not protected by Title VII.)

2. **Review the Workplace Anti- Discrimination Policy:**

Most employers will provide a copy of the Workplace Anti-Discrimination Policy in the Employee Handbook. Read and understand the Workplace Anti-Discrimination Policy. If you have questions or concerns, contact your supervisor or human resources manager.

3. **Research State and Federal Employment Laws:**

Understand federal and state laws related to employment discrimination. Federal employment legislation such as Title VII and state employment discrimination statutes are available online, in law libraries, or in public libraries. Remember that the terms natural hairstyles and protective hairstyles may be interchangeable.

4. **Research the EEOC and State Employment Discrimination Agencies**:

The EEOC enforces Title VII or federal employment discrimination laws. State employment discrimination agencies enforce state employment discrimination laws. The EEOC and state employment discrimination agencies investigate discrimination charges based on race, which includes natural hair and other physical characteristics.

5. **Contact an Employment Discrimination Law Attorney**:

If you have questions about employment discrimination law, contact an attorney in your state. You can get attorney referrals from the state and local bar associations. The American Bar Association also provides links to state and local bar associations.

Biography

Tracy Sanders, Esq. is an accomplished attorney, author, and speaker. Ms. Sanders established Natural Hair and the Law, an organization formed to provide publications, workshops, and events addressing legal issues related to natural hair in the workplace and schools. Ms. Sanders is author of *"Natural Hair in the Workplace: What Are Your Rights?,"* which has been featured in *Black Caucus of the American Library Association, Essence, Los Angeles Sentinel, Naturally Curly, New Growth Magazine*, and *Top 100 Magazine.* She also wrote another book, *"Natural Hair Affirmations."* The books are available for purchase online at Barnes and Noble. Ms. Sanders received numerous prestigious awards. She was honored with a *Certificate of Special Recognition* from United States Congresswoman Karen Bass for outstanding community service at *Extraordinary Women Rock*. Ms. Sanders is a recipient of *Comerica Bank Los Angeles Lakers Women's Business Awards* and *Angels in Red Awards.* Additionally, she was a featured speaker at *Alpha Kappa Alpha Sorority Leadership Seminar, Arizona State University Sandra Day O'Connor College of Law, Corporate Counsel Women of Color, and Thurgood Marshall School of Law.* Ms. Sanders made appearances on TV networks such as *ABC, Fox, MSNBC, TLC,* and *WE.* Ms. Sanders obtained a Bachelor of Arts degree in Political Science from the University of South Carolina, Master of Public Administration degree from the University of South Carolina, and Juris Doctorate degree from Syracuse University School of Law. She is a member of the American Bar Association, American Society for Public Administration, and Black Women Lawyers Association of Los Angeles. Ms. Sanders attributes her success to a passion for promoting liberty, empowerment, and social justice.

Natural Hair and the Law®
Tracy Sanders, Esq.

Made in the USA
Monee, IL
12 April 2021

64483798R00036